BASS BUILDERS
HIP-HOP BASS

101 GROOVES, RIFFS, LOOPS, AND BEATS

PLAYBACK+
Speed • Pitch • Balance • Loop

To access audio visit:
www.halleonard.com/mylibrary

5905-9491-8486-4557

CONTENTS

ISBN 978-0-634-02296-8

HAL•LEONARD®
7777 W. BLUEMOUND RD. P.O. BOX 13819 MILWAUKEE, WI 53213

Visit Hal Leonard Online at
www.halleonard.com

INTRODUCTION

Hip-hop music was born in the mid '70s on the streets of New York City and soon found its way into the studios of such pioneers as the Bomb Squad, Public Enemy, the Sugar Hill Gang, and Grandmaster Flash and the Furious Five. In the early '80s, the style spilled over into the streets of Los Angeles, and, with the help of artists such as N.W.A., Dr. Dre, and DJ Yellow, "West Coast" style was born. Soon after, the movement spread to various parts of the country—including "down South" with artists like Outcast and 2 Live Crew.

Without getting into its culture and fashion, the best way to define hip-hop music would be to call it an urban form not necessarily originated by live musicians playing their instruments together, but rather by assembling and overlapping various rhythms, samples, sounds, and musical lines. This collage, also known as a "beat," is then used as background for either a rap or a melody.

Categorizing sub-styles of a music like hip-hop, which is mostly driven by borrowed samples of pre-existing songs, is not easy. By now, the task is further complicated in that the various sub-styles have influenced each other. A basic geographical breakdown of hip-hop would look like this:

- East Coast: more sample-driven
- West Coast: a bit more laid back, bass-driven, and more "performed"
- Down South (also known as "Dirty South"): more active, with quick hi-hats, heavy snares, heavy kick drums, and overall "trashier" sounds.

A big part of hip-hop music is the bass guitar and the use of bass lines previously heard in early Motown or '70s funk. A good example is the Sugar Hill Gang's "Rapper's Delight," the first hip-hop tune to achieve commercial radio success in the early '80s. The background track of this song is rooted in the extremely strong bass line of Chic's Top 10 hit "Good Times."

The best way to teach a musical style that is derivative of bass lines originating from '60s and '70s funk is through performance. I am a firm believer that if you learn enough vocabulary, you will be able to speak the language. Thus, rather than trying to explain hip-hop bass playing, I chose to perform 101 bass lines that cover twenty years of hip-hop music, and then transcribed each example. The book is divided into three sections: 1) East Coast, 2) West Coast, and 3) Down South. Have fun, and good luck.

— *Josquin des Prés*

Special thanks to producer Jacob Smythe (p.k.a. "Boxxcutter") and artist Russell A. Pryor (p.k.a. D.Kompose) for their insight into the origins of hip-hop music.

Recorded at Track Star Studios, La Mesa, CA. Loops and beats by Tristan des Prés.

About the Author

Born in St. Tropez, France, Josquin des Prés is a world-renowned bassist who has shared credits with such players as Jeff Porcaro, Steve Lukather, Vinnie Colaiuta, Billy Sheehan, Bunny Brunel, Jimmy Crespo, David Garibadi, Alex Acuna, and Jerry Goodman, among others. Many of his bass lines can be heard on various hip-hop loops sample CDs. In addition to his career as a bass player, Josquin des Pres is the author of twelve bass instruction and music reference books, as well as an accomplished producer and songwriter, with production credits on over 40 CDs and numerous songs covered by international artists, including multiple collaborations with Elton John's lyricist Bernie Taupin.

East Coast Patterns

Pattern 1

Pattern 2

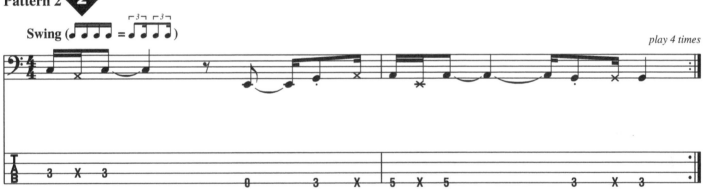

Pattern 3

Pattern 4

Pattern 5

Swing

Pattern 6

Swing

play 4 times

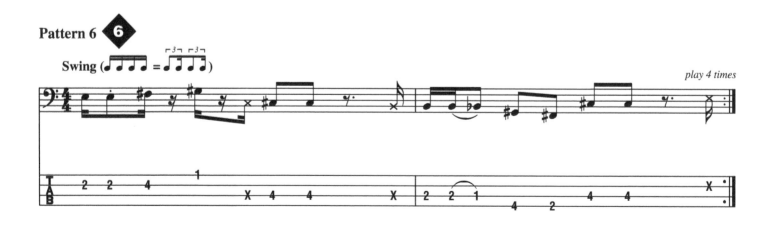

Pattern 7

Pattern 8

Pattern 9

Pattern 10

Pattern 11

Pattern 12

Pattern 13

Pattern 14

Pattern 15

Pattern 16

Pattern 17

Pattern 18

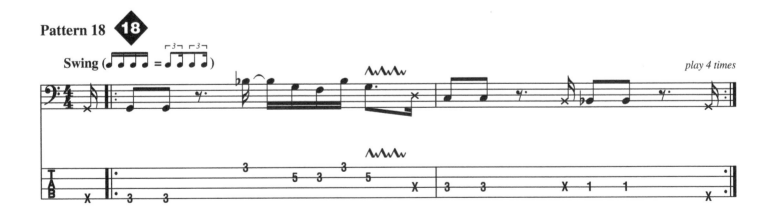

Pattern 19

Pattern 20

Pattern 21

Pattern 22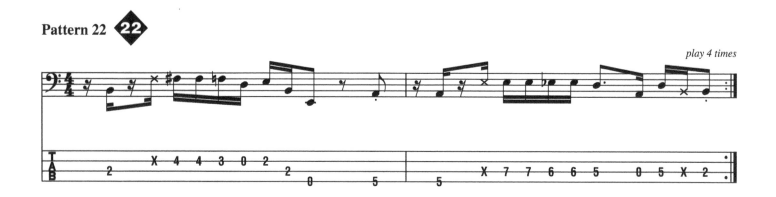

Pattern 23

Pattern 24

Pattern 25

Pattern 26

Pattern 27

Pattern 28

Pattern 29

Pattern 30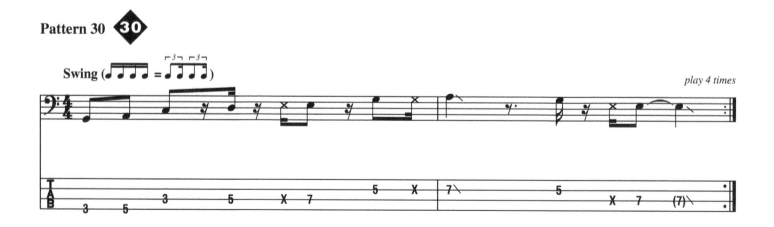

West Coast Patterns

Pattern 31 31

Pattern 32 32

Pattern 33 33

Pattern 34 34

Pattern 35

Pattern 36

Pattern 37

Pattern 38

play 4 times

Pattern 39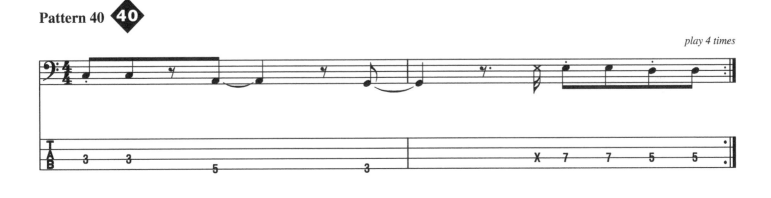

play 4 times

Pattern 40

play 4 times

Pattern 41

play 4 times

Pattern 42

Pattern 43

Pattern 44

Pattern 45

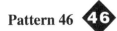

Pattern 46

play 3 times

Pattern 47

play 4 times

Pattern 48

Swing

play 4 times

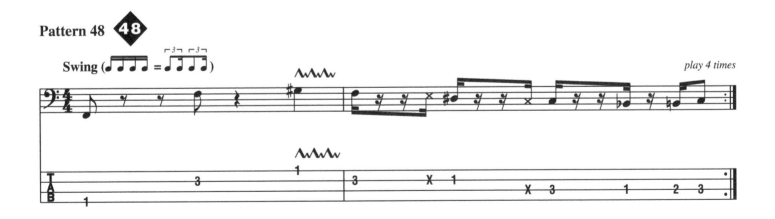

Pattern 49

Pattern 50

Pattern 51

Pattern 52

Pattern 53

Pattern 54

Pattern 55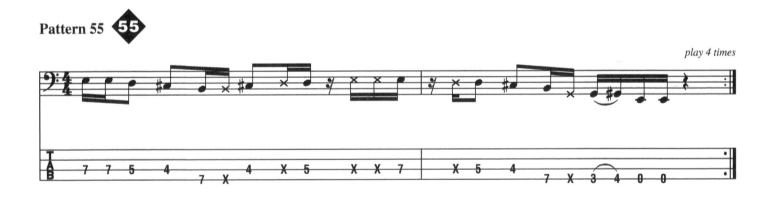

Pattern 56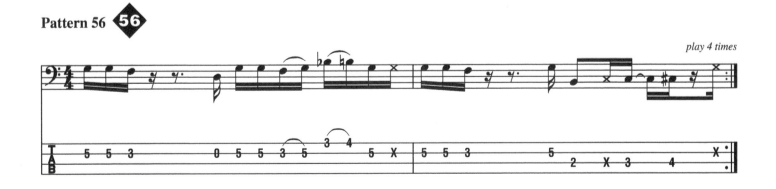

17

Pattern 57

play 4 times

Pattern 58

play 4 times

Pattern 59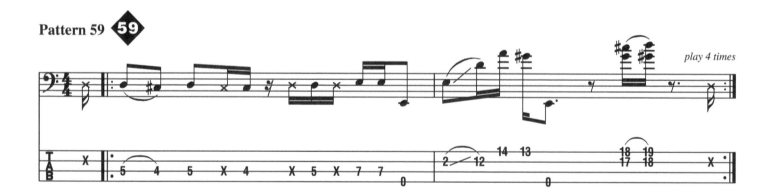

play 4 times

Pattern 60

play 4 times

Pattern 61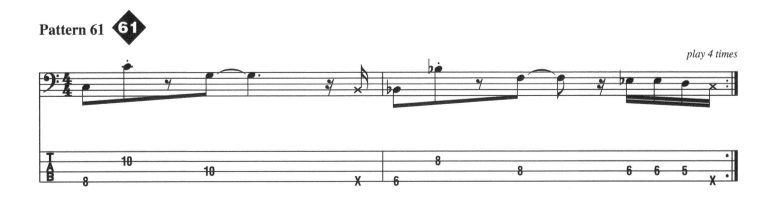

Pattern 62

Pattern 63

Pattern 64

19

Pattern 65 65

Swing

play 4 times

Pattern 66 66

Swing

play 4 times

Pattern 67 67

play 4 times

Pattern 68 68

play 4 times

Down South Patterns

Pattern 69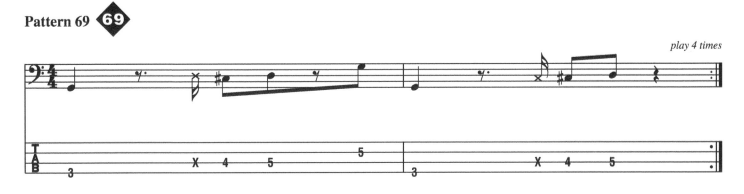

Pattern 70

Pattern 71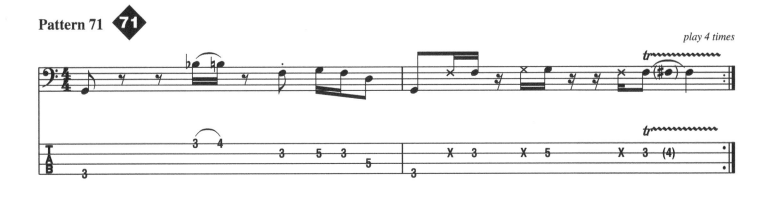

Pattern 72

Pattern 73

play 4 times

Pattern 74

Pattern 75

play 4 times

Pattern 76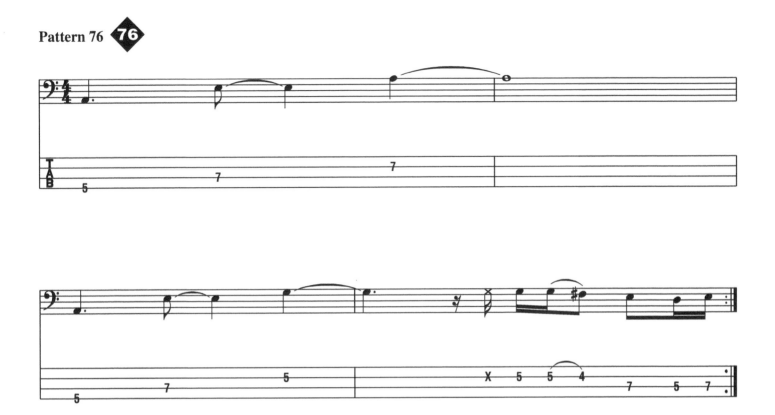

Pattern 77

Pattern 78

Pattern 79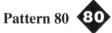

Pattern 80 80

Pattern 81 81

Pattern 82 82

Pattern 83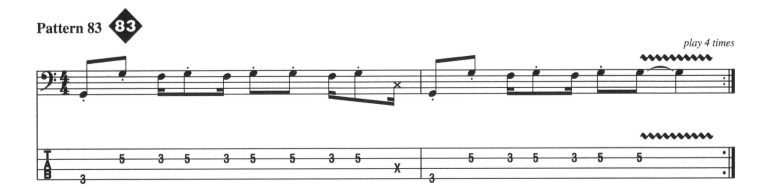

play 4 times

Pattern 84

play 4 times

Pattern 85

play 4 times

Pattern 86

play 4 times

Pattern 87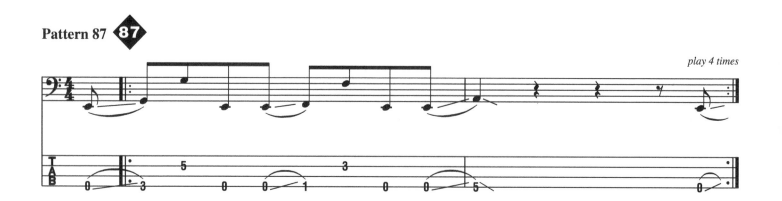

Pattern 88

Pattern 89

Pattern 90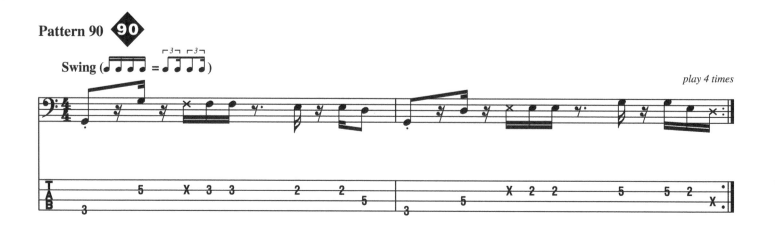

Pattern 91

Pattern 92

Pattern 93

Pattern 94

Pattern 95

Pattern 96

Pattern 97

Pattern 98

*Track 98 also includes Patterns 99, 100, and 101.

Pattern 99

Pattern 100

play 4 times

Pattern 101

play 4 times

Bass Notation Legend

Bass music can be notated two different ways: on a *musical staff*, and in *tablature*.

THE MUSICAL STAFF shows pitches and rhythms and is divided by bar lines into measures. Pitches are named after the first seven letters of the alphabet.

TABLATURE graphically represents the bass fingerboard. Each horizontal line represents a string, and each number represents a fret.

Notes:

Strings:

3rd string, open   2nd string, 2nd fret   1st & 2nd strings open, played together

HAMMER-ON: Strike the first (lower) note with one finger, then sound the higher note (on the same string) with another finger by fretting it without picking.

PULL-OFF: Place both fingers on the notes to be sounded. Strike the first note and without picking, pull the finger off to sound the second (lower) note.

LEGATO SLIDE: Strike the first note and then slide the same fret-hand finger up or down to the second note. The second note is not struck.

SHIFT SLIDE: Same as legato slide, except the second note is struck.

TRILL: Very rapidly alternate between the notes indicated by continuously hammering on and pulling off.

TREMOLO PICKING: The note is picked as rapidly and continuously as possible.

VIBRATO: The string is vibrated by rapidly bending and releasing the note with the fretting hand.

SHAKE: Using one finger, rapidly alternate between two notes on one string by sliding either a half-step above or below.

NATURAL HARMONIC: Strike the note while the fret hand lightly touches the string directly over the fret indicated.

Harm.

MUFFLED STRINGS: A percussive sound is produced by laying the fret hand across the string(s) without depressing them and striking them with the pick hand.

BEND: Strike the note and bend up the interval shown.

1/2

BEND AND RELEASE: Strike the note and bend up as indicated, then release back to the original note. Only the first note is struck.

1/2

RIGHT-HAND TAP: Hammer ("tap") the fret indicated with the "pick-hand" index or middle finger and pull off to the note fretted by the fret hand.

+

LEFT-HAND TAP: Hammer ("tap") the fret indicated with the "fret-hand" index or middle finger.

SLAP: Strike ("slap") string with right-hand thumb.

T

POP: Snap ("pop") string with right-hand index or middle finger.

P

Additional Musical Definitions

>	(accent)	• Accentuate note (play it louder)
∧	(accent)	• Accentuate note with great intensity
•	(staccato)	• Play the note short
⊓		• Downstroke
∨		• Upstroke

D.S. al Coda   • Go back to the sign (𝄋), then play until the measure marked "***To Coda***," then skip to the section labelled "***Coda***."

D.C. al Fine   • Go back to the beginning of the song and play until the measure marked "***Fine***" (end).

Bass Fig.   • Label used to recall a recurring pattern.

Fill   • Label used to identify a brief pattern which is to be inserted into the arrangement.

tacet   • Instrument is silent (drops out).

• Repeat measures between signs.

| 1. | 2. | • When a repeated section has different endings, play the first ending only the first time and the second ending only the second time. |

NOTE: Tablature numbers in parentheses mean:
1. The note is being sustained over a system (note in standard notation is tied), or
2. The note is sustained, but a new articulation (such as a hammer-on, pull-off, slide or vibrato begins, or
3. The note is a barely audible "ghost" note (note in standard notation is also in parentheses).

BASS BUILDERS

A series of technique book/audio packages created for the purposeful building and development of your chops. Each volume is written by an expert in that particular technique. And with the inclusion of audio, the added dimension of hearing exactly how to play particular grooves and techniques make these truly like private lessons.

BASS FOR BEGINNERS
by Glenn Letsch
00695099 Book/CD Pack.................................... $19.95

BASS GROOVES
by Jon Liebman
00696028 Book/Online Audio $19.99

BASS IMPROVISATION
by Ed Friedland
00695164 Book/Online Audio $19.99

BLUES BASS
by Jon Liebman
00695235 Book/Online Audio $19.99

BUILDING WALKING BASS LINES
by Ed Friedland
00695008 Book/Online Audio $19.99

RON CARTER –
BUILDING JAZZ BASS LINES
00841240 Book/Online Audio $19.99

DICTIONARY OF BASS GROOVES
by Sean Malone
00695266 Book/Online Audio $14.95

EXPANDING WALKING BASS LINES
by Ed Friedland
00695026 Book/Online Audio $19.99

FINGERBOARD HARMONY FOR BASS
by Gary Willis
00695043 Book/Online Audio $17.99

FUNK BASS
by Jon Liebman
00699348 Book/Online Audio $19.99

FUNK/FUSION BASS
by Jon Liebman
00696553 Book/Online Audio $24.99

HIP-HOP BASS
by Josquin des Prés
00695589 Book/Online Audio $15.99

JAZZ BASS
by Ed Friedland
00695084 Book/Online Audio $17.99

JERRY JEMMOTT –
BLUES AND RHYTHM &
BLUES BASS TECHNIQUE
00695176 Book/CD Pack.................................... $24.99

JUMP 'N' BLUES BASS
by Keith Rosier
00695292 Book/Online Audio $17.99

THE LOST ART OF COUNTRY BASS
by Keith Rosier
00695107 Book/Online Audio $19.99

PENTATONIC SCALES FOR BASS
by Ed Friedland
00696224 Book/Online Audio $19.99

REGGAE BASS
by Ed Friedland
00695163 Book/Online Audio $16.99

'70S FUNK & DISCO BASS
by Josquin des Prés
00695614 Book/Online Audio $16.99

SIMPLIFIED SIGHT-READING
FOR BASS
by Josquin des Prés
00695085 Book/Online Audio $17.99

6-STRING BASSICS
by David Gross
00695221 Book/Online Audio $14.99

HAL•LEONARD®

halleonard.com

Prices, contents and availability subject to change without notice; All prices are listed in U.S. funds

HAL·LEONARD® BASS PLAY-ALONG

The Bass Play-Along™ Series will help you play your favorite songs quickly and easily! Just follow the tab, listen to the audio to hear how the bass should sound, and then play-along using the separate backing tracks. The melody and lyrics are also included in the book in case you want to sing, or to simply help you follow along. The audio files are enhanced so you can adjust the recording to any tempo without changing pitch!

HAL·LEONARD®

Prices, contents, and availability subject to change without notice.

Visit Hal Leonard Online at **www.halleonard.com**